Why Do My Feet Fall Asleep?

and other questions about the circulatory system

by

Sharon Cromwell

Photographs by

Richard Smolinski, Jr.

Series Consultant

Dan Hogan

RIGBY INTERACTIVE LIBRARY
DES PLAINES, ILLINOIS

© 1998 Reed Educational & Professional Publishing
Published by Rigby Interactive Library,
an imprint of Reed Educational & Professional Publishing,
1350 East Touhy Avenue, Suite 240 West
Des Plaines, IL 60018

02 01 00 99 98
10 9 8 7 6 5 4 3 2 1

Produced by Times Offset (M) Sdn. Bhd.

Library of Congress Cataloging-in-Publication Data

Cromwell, Sharon, 1947-
    Why do my feet fall asleep? : and other questions about the circulatory system / by Sharon Cromwell ; photographs by Richard Smolinski, Jr.
        p.   cm. -- (Bodywise)
    Includes bibliographical references and index.
    Summary: Describes how the human circulatory system works and discusses such related topics as blood pressure, bruising, and shivering.
        ISBN 1-57572-162-7 (lib. bdg.)
        1. Cardiovascular system--Physiology--Juvenile literature.
    [1. Circulatory system.]   I. Smolinski, Dick, ill. II. Title. III. Series.
    QP103.C76   1997
    612.1--dc21   97-22213
                                                                            CIP
                                                                            AC

Some words are shown in bold, **like this.** You can find out what they mean by looking in the glossary.

Contents

What is my circulatory system?   4

What keeps my blood moving around?   6

Why do I have blood?   8

What makes my heart beat?   10

What is blood pressure?   12

Why do I shiver when I'm cold?   14

Why do my feet fall asleep?   16

Why do I sweat when I get hot?   18

What makes bruises "black and blue"?   20

EXPLORE MORE! Your Circulatory System   22

Glossary   *24*

More Books to Read   *24*

Index   *24*

What is *my circulatory system?*

Your body is made up of **cells**. To work, these cells need a constant supply of **oxygen** and **nutrients**. These are carried by the blood. Blood moves through your body all the time. Your heart acts like a pump and keeps the blood moving.

Your blood and your heart are part of your circulatory system. This system circulates, or moves, your blood to all parts of your body. The blood moves through tubes called blood vessels. There are three kinds of blood vessels—arteries, veins, and capillaries.

HEALTH FACT

There is something in your body called cholesterol. Some of it may come from eating fatty foods. Too much cholesterol can make it difficult for your blood vessels to carry blood through your body.

Blood without oxygen

Blood with oxygen

Artery

Vein

Heart

Lungs

What keeps my blood moving around?

Your heart sends blood with a lot of **oxygen** in it through your arteries. From your arteries, the blood travels through many capillaries—these are narrow blood vessels with thin walls that reach all of the parts of your body.

Oxygen and **nutrients** pass through the capillary walls to reach the **cells** in your body that need them. Then the blood— which has lost most of its oxygen—picks up **waste** from your cells. Much of that waste is a **gas** called carbon dioxide.

From your capillaries, the blood travels back to your heart through your veins. Next, the blood goes on a short trip to the lungs, where the blood gives up its carbon dioxide and takes in more oxygen. Then the process begins all over again.

HEALTH FACT
After you jump rope for a while, you begin to breathe hard. This helps your body get the extra oxygen that it needs when you exercise.

Why do I have blood?

Blood carries **oxygen** through your body and fights sickness in your body.

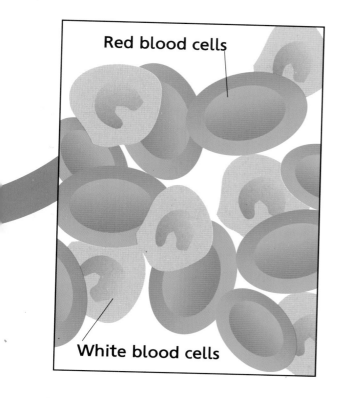

Red blood cells

White blood cells

3. Red blood cells bring oxygen from your lungs to your body's cells. They also carry carbon dioxide, a **waste** product, away from your cells.

4. White blood cells fight sickness in your body. They are part of what is called your **immune system**. You only need white blood cells from time to time. That's why you have fewer of them than red blood cells.

1. Your blood **cells** are made in the large bones of your body.

2. Your blood has two kinds of blood cells, red and white.

What makes my heart beat?

Your heartbeat is produced by electrical signals that come from inside your heart.

HEALTH FACT

Regular exercise makes your heart muscle stronger and larger. It does not have to beat as much as the heart of someone who doesn't exercise.

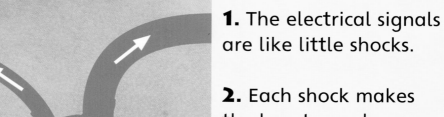

1. The electrical signals are like little shocks.

2. Each shock makes the heart muscle tighten and then loosen.

Heart

3. When the muscle squeezes together, blood is forced out into your arteries and through your body.

4. When the muscle relaxes, your heart fills with blood.

5. Your heartbeat is when the heart muscle relaxes and then squeezes together.

What is blood pressure?

Blood pressure is the force of blood pushing against the walls of your arteries. This pressure can be measured.

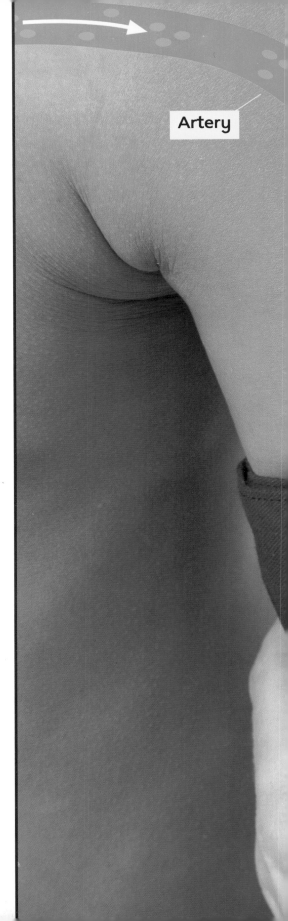

Artery

HEALTH FACT

Eating a lot of salty food can make your blood pressure go up. Older adults who have high blood pressure are more likely to have heart disease.

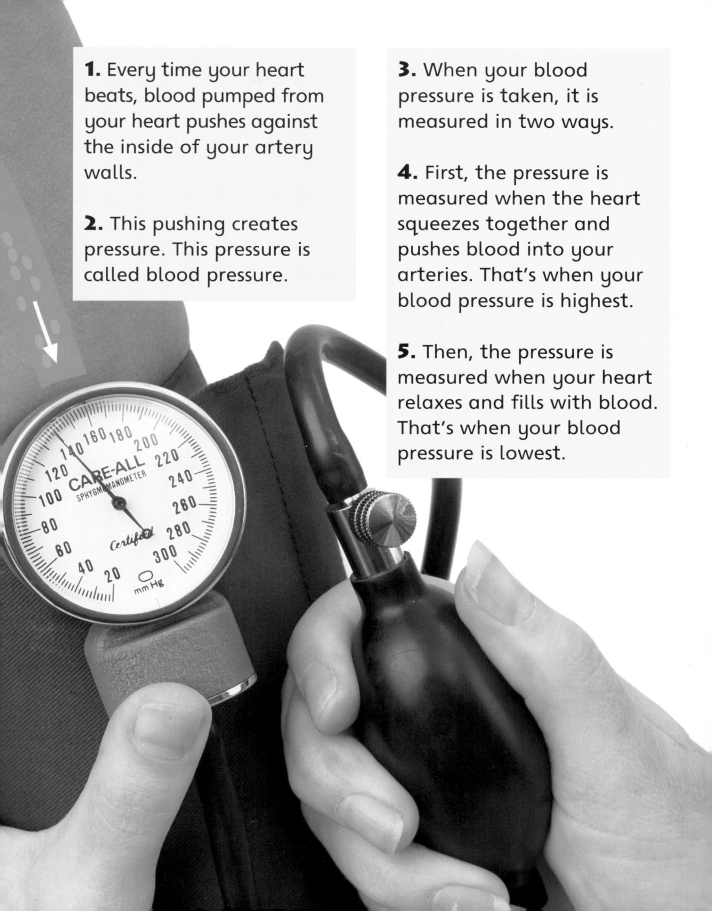

1. Every time your heart beats, blood pumped from your heart pushes against the inside of your artery walls.

2. This pushing creates pressure. This pressure is called blood pressure.

3. When your blood pressure is taken, it is measured in two ways.

4. First, the pressure is measured when the heart squeezes together and pushes blood into your arteries. That's when your blood pressure is highest.

5. Then, the pressure is measured when your heart relaxes and fills with blood. That's when your blood pressure is lowest.

Why do I shiver when I'm cold?

Shivering is your body's way of trying to warm up.

HEALTH FACT

You can't catch a cold just from getting chilled. But a chill makes it harder for your body to fight off germs.

1. When your body becomes cold, your circulatory system does not send out as much blood to your arms and legs. Instead, it keeps more of your blood near your heart, lungs, and other important **organs**. This helps your organs stay warm.

2. Your arms and legs warm themselves when you shiver. This shaking and shivering happens when the muscles in your arms and legs squeeze together.

3. As your muscles squeeze tightly, this action makes you shake and shiver.

4. This shaking and shivering releases energy, just as exercise does.

5. The energy that is released produces heat and warms you up!

6. But shivering only warms you up for a short time.

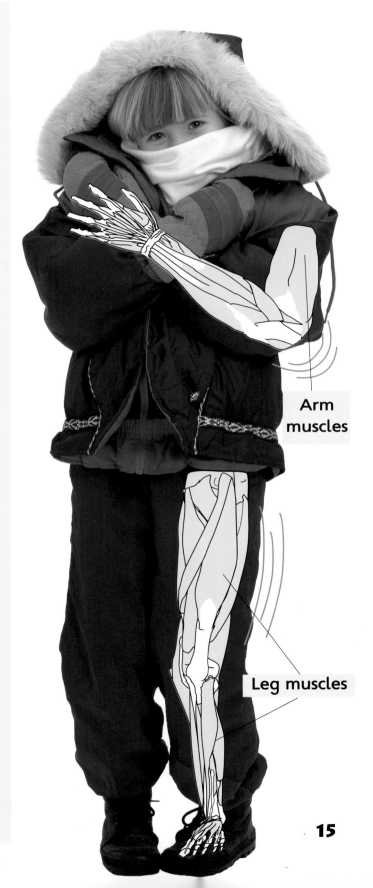

Arm muscles

Leg muscles

15

Why do my feet fall asleep?

Your feet fall asleep when there is less blood flowing to them.

HEALTH FACT

If your fingers and toes feel cold all the time, it may be a sign of poor circulation. This means not enough blood is reaching them.

1. When you put weight on your feet or don't move for a while, less blood flows to them.

2. Your feet's nerves are also squashed. These are long, thin body parts that let you feel things.

3. When less blood flows into your feet, less **oxygen** is carried there.

4. When less blood and oxygen flow to a body part, like a foot, the muscles of that body part get weak.

5. The squashed nerves also begin to lose their feeling.

6. These things make the body part feel as if it's "asleep." When the body part moves again, the nerves go back to their normal shape, and blood rushes to the body part. It "wakes up" with sharp stabs that feel like needles.

Blood vessels

Nerves

Why do I sweat when I get hot?

Sweating is part of your body's cooling system.

HEALTH FACT

Many experts say that to keep fit, you should exercise until you're breathing hard for at least 20 minutes. You should do this at least 3 times a week.

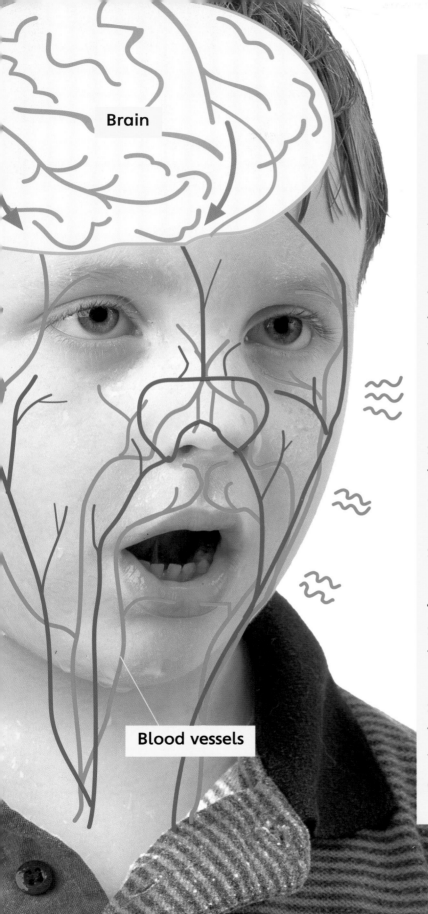

Brain

Blood vessels

1. Your blood vessels carry heat from deep inside your body to your skin.

2. When you're hot, your brain sends messages to the blood vessels in your skin, telling them to open wider.

3. As the heat is released through your skin, it gets cooled by the outside air. This quick cooling creates liquid, also known as sweat.

4. The sweat on your skin's surface also helps to cool your body. This happens when the sweat evaporates. It turns from liquid into a vapor, like the steam of a boiling pot of water.

19

What makes bruises "black and blue"?

A bruise, or "black-and-blue" mark, is caused when capillaries, or tiny blood vessels, are broken underneath your skin.

HEALTH FACT

When you have a bruise, try holding ice against it. The ice reduces the amount of blood flowing to the skin. With less blood flowing to the wounded part, there is less swelling.

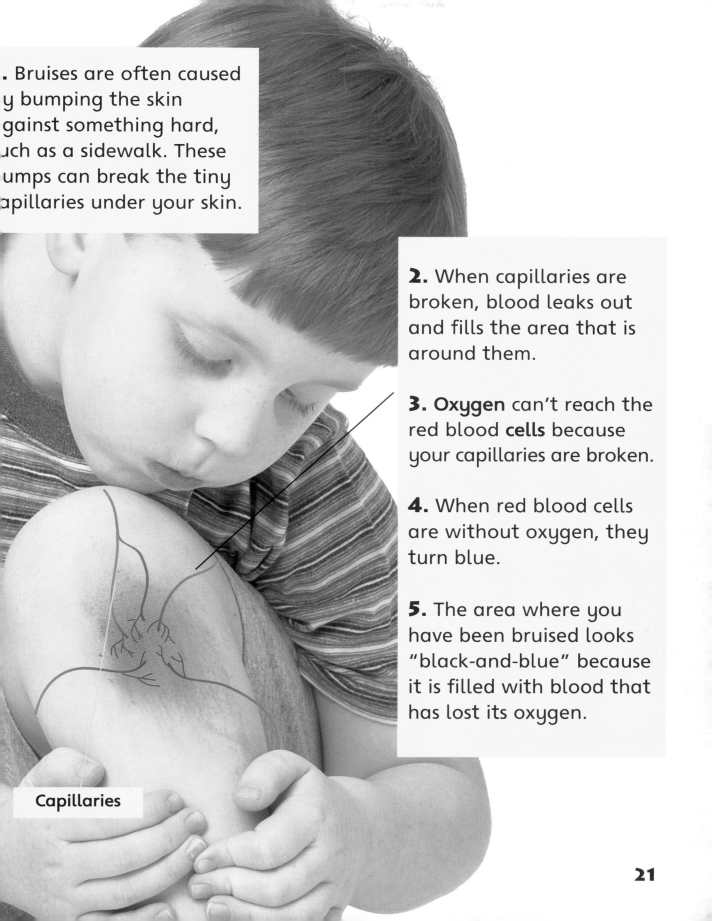

. Bruises are often caused
y bumping the skin
gainst something hard,
uch as a sidewalk. These
umps can break the tiny
apillaries under your skin.

2. When capillaries are broken, blood leaks out and fills the area that is around them.

3. Oxygen can't reach the red blood **cells** because your capillaries are broken.

4. When red blood cells are without oxygen, they turn blue.

5. The area where you have been bruised looks "black-and-blue" because it is filled with blood that has lost its oxygen.

Capillaries

EXPLORE MORE!
Your Circulatory System

1. BEAT THE CLOCK!
WHAT YOU'LL NEED:
- a sports watch or stopwatch
- a cardboard tube (paper towel roll or something similar)
- a friend to help you

THEN TRY THIS!
Work with a friend to learn about your heart. Place a cardboard tube against your friend's back with your ear at the other end. While your friend watches the second hand on the clock, count the number of times his or her heart beats in 30 seconds. Double the number to find out how many times your friend's heart beats per minute. This is your friend's resting pulse. Then switch places with your friend so he or she can figure out your resting pulse. Write down both your friend's and your own resting pulses.

Next take turns with your friend running in place for 30 seconds. When one stops running, the other one should take the pulse. Measure your heartbeats per minute. Write down the heartbeats after running for both you and your friend. After you and your friend finish, look at the numbers you have written down. Which number is the highest? Why do you think that is?

2. GO WITH THE FLOW!

WHAT YOU'LL NEED:
- a garden hose
- a small, light object, such as a styrofoam ball. It should fit easily inside the hose.
- water

THEN TRY THIS!
This activity will show you how blood circulates through your body. Take any removable parts—such as a nozzle—off both sides of the hose. At the faucet end, place your small object inside the hose. Then attach that end to the faucet. Leave the other end of the hose open. Turn on the water just a little bit and look at the open end of the hose. Did your object get pushed through? Then turn the water up all the way. Now do you see your object? The garden hose is like your arteries, veins, and capillaries. The water inside is like your blood. The object moving through shows you how blood moves **oxygen** throughout your body. Turning the water on low and then high shows you the difference between low and high blood pressure.

Glossary

cells Very small parts of a person, animal, or plant.

gas A substance, such as air, that isn't solid or liquid, that spreads to fill the space it is in.

immune system The parts of your body that work together to fight disease.

nutrients The things in food that keep you healthy and help you grow.

organ A part of the body that does one job.

oxygen A colorless **gas** that is in the air. We need oxygen to breathe.

waste Something left over that isn't needed by the body.

More Books to Read

Bailey, Donna. *All about the Heart and Blood.* Chatham, NJ: Raintree Steck-Vaughn, 1990.

Bryan, Jenny. *The Pulse of Life: The Circulatory System.* Morristown, NJ: Silver Burdett Press.

Parker, Steve. *The Heart and Blood.* Danbury, CT: Franklin Watts, 1991.

Paramon, Merce. *How Our Blood Circulates.* New York: Chelsea House, 1994.

Silverstein, Alvin. *Circulatory System.* New York: 21st Century Books, 1994.

Index

arteries, 4, 6, 11, 12
blood, purpose of, 8
blood cells, 9
blood pressure, 12–13
blood vessels, 4, 6, 11, 12, 20
body temperature, regulation of, 14–15, 18–19
bruising, 20–21
carbon dioxide, 6, 9
capillaries, 4, 6, 20
cells, 4, 6, 9
circulation, lack of, 16–17
heart, 4, 10–11
immune system, 9
nerves, 17
nutrients, 4, 6
oxygen, 4, 6, 8, 9, 17
red blood cells, 9
shivering, 14–15
sweating, 18–19
veins, 4, 6
white blood cells, 9